Authors

Elizabeth (Betsy) Bragg and Celia Elinson

Editor

Heike Westphal

Cover and Book Design

Celia Elinson

Food Photography

Kathleen Bryce

Cover and Children's Photography

Miryam Wiley

Photos

FreeDigitalPhotos.net, iStock, Flickr

ISBN: 978-1-5032-2465-0

Table of Content

Acknowledgements

We would like to offer special thanks to all the children in the Real Kids Real Food afterschool program at the Mystic Learning Center, 530 Mystic Avenue, Somerville MA. These children prepared, tested and highly recommended the recipes in this book. We also greatly appreciate the contribution of the staff members, interns, and passionate volunteers of Real Kids Real Food. Furthermore, we are very grateful for our many talented generous raw vegan chefs, who have provided delicious healthful recipes to Real Kids Real Food, Kids-tested Recipes.

About the Authors

Elizabeth (Betsy) Bragg

Her passion and mission is to prevent obesity, chronic disease and malnutrition in children, through education and advocacy of healthy living. This sprang from her life changing experiences at the Hippocrates Health Institute (HHI) in West Palm Beach, Florida. Crippled from arthritis and substance abuse, Betsy was gifted by her son with the HHI three-week transformational life program, which healed her and inspired her to become certified as an HHI Health Educator.

Now revitalized, at 80 years of age, Betsy is Executive Director of the non-profit Optimum Health Solution and founder of Real Kids Real Food, a healthy afterschool program for at risk, low income, inner-city children ages 5 – 12.

Betsy's background includes being a Director of the Middlesex County Employment and Training Program for Refugees and Immigrants; a teacher from kindergarten through college; a principal of Lindsley Associates working on economic and social programs with the United Nations, USAID and Central American Bank in the West Indies, the Philippines, Japan and El Salvador. Her varied background also includes being a career counselor for students, the unemployed and the disabled, computer consultant, and chef.

Betsy received her Bachelor's degree from Smith College in History and English, a Master's in Counseling and Education from Stanford University and Harvard University, a Master's in Education from Boston University in the Administration of Multi-Cultural Non Profit Organizations and a Certificate as a Hippocrates Health Educator.

www.OptimumHealthSolution.org; www.RealKidsRealFood.org

Celia Elinson

Her mission is to help people of all ages achieve vibrant health and happiness with a style that is both fun and easy to follow. Her approach is based on the Hippocrates Health Institute in West Palm Beach, Florida living food lifestyle, which focuses on an organic, raw food, such as sprouts, green juices, vegetables, sea vegetables, grains, nuts and seeds. This inspired her to complete the Eat to Thrive Health Educator course and to become a certified Health Educator.

Her philosophy is quite simple: be smart what you eat, integrate healthy and nutritious whole foods into your diet, while developing new habits that will last for a lifetime.

Celia is a volunteer teacher for Real Kids Real Food, the Optimum Health Solution's after school program for at risk, low income, inner-city children ages 5 -12.

Her background includes being a Manager in a Dental Laboratory, a Translator and Customer Service Associate at Hippocrates Health Institute.

Celia's education includes a Bachelor's degree from a Beltsy University in former USSR.

Heike Westphal, Editor

Heike's mission is to ease the transition to a life enriching raw vegan lifestyle.

In 2010, still breast-feeding, Heike was diagnosed with stage 3b breast cancer, went through chemotherapy, mastectomy and radiation, that put the cancer in remission.

She believed that if she didn't change her lifestyle, cancer would return. Therefore, she looked for a new approach to detoxify from the treatments, build a strong immune system and stay energized to keep up with her four-year-old daughter. She discovered the Hippocrates Health Institute and attended the three-week Life Transformation program. It took her to a completely new level of health. Returning from Hippocrates, she learned to practice the living food lifestyle by attending the "Eat to Thrive 10-week Life Long Healthy Habits & Healthy Living Lifestyle" course. It was time to say goodbye to her husband's delicious meals, mostly based on meat with few greens and get creative in the kitchen herself.

A compact sprout and wheat grass garden is now a feature in their city apartment. Her daughter enjoys being the sprout fairy; planting and watering, and most importantly, eating the sprouts.

Now, there are two chefs in Heike's kitchen and the two worlds coexist very well. Their daughter gravitates to raw vegan meals and Heike is still working on her husband's taste buds.

Kathleen Bryce, Photographer

She is an oil painter and photographer who often depicts food as her subject matter. Her studio and kitchen are laboratories for creativity. She is a food stylist and chef interested in the healing properties of food. Bryce Studios was founded in 2010.

Foreword

Real Kids Real Food is a work of love for the most precious among us. Raising four children and now grand parenting four, I have personally experienced over four decades the powerful effect that food has on the development, health, and psyche of our children.

Betsy Bragg and Celia Elinson have penned a contribution that will offer a powerful foundation to raise children on. Their own lives were transformed by embracing real food. Food chemistry at Hippocrates, the father of western medicine, states "it is a medicine".

In 1975 I began my professional life direction at a natural health center in Stockholm, Sweden. We utilized organic plant-based cuisine, validated and watched the miraculous effect it has on reversing and preventing disease. Cutting edge research today revealed that these unpolluted plant fare are filled with phytochemicals that selectively and effectively target and kill a plethora of illnesses.

Hippocrates Health Institute, which I am honored to co-direct, has been on the forefront of plant-based medicine for 60 years and clinically has established a body of science that supports this fare significantly. Future medicine will in great part be based on lifestyle and epigenetics. Do not wait for the research to be published, embrace these foods and inherent strength so that you and your children can begin receiving its healing power.

Dr. Anna Maria Clement, PhD, NMD, LN
Co-Director, The Hippocrates Health Institute
and author of *Healthful Cuisine*

Introduction Real Kids Real Food

Through hands-on activities concerning nutrition, local and organic food, farming and gardening, grocery shopping, planning and preparing meals, children learn how to achieve and continue an overall healthy lifestyle. The program broadens their exposure to making healthy choices with attention to affordability and incorporates physical activities and parent involvement throughout the year. Optimum Health Solution has piloted this program in other public housing environments with measurable success.

Real Kids in Action

Cool Tools for Raw Chefs

Measuring Cups

Measuring Spoons

Cutting Boards

Peeler

Food Processor

High-Speed Blender

Lemon/Lime Juicer

Mixing Bowls

11

Rubber spatula

Forks, knifes, spoons

Mandolin

Dehydrator

Spiralizer

Food Preparation Tips

Buying Tips

- Purchase produce that is not bruised or damaged.
- Choose items that are refrigerated when selecting fresh-cut produce.

Preparation Tips

- Wash your hands with warm water and soap before and after preparing fresh produce.
- Cut away any damaged or bruised areas on fruits and vegetables.
- Discard produce that looks rotten.
- Wash fruits and vegetables under running water.
- Scrub produce, such as melons and cucumbers, with a clean produce brush.
- Dry produce to reduce bacteria that may be present.
- Follow the recipe step-by-step and measure carefully.
- Avoid using sharp knives with young children; use sturdy plastic knives.
- Use hand juicers to squeeze citrus fruit.

Storage Tips

- Store perishable fresh fruits and vegetables (like strawberries, lettuce, herbs, and mushrooms) in a clean refrigerator at a temperature of 40° F or below.
- Refrigerate all produce that is purchased pre-cut or peeled.

Thoughts for Parents

- Eat with your children to set an example.
- Be enthusiastic and positive about the meal.
- Eat at least five servings of colorful fruits and vegetables to get wide range of vitamins, minerals and proteins.
- Show good behavior, which is essential for growing children.
- Post healthy snack list on your refrigerator door.
- Be patient with new foods.
- Encourage your children to talk about the shape, color, and texture of food.
- Introduce new fruits and vegetables each week.
- Visit farms and farmer's market.
- Plant a garden.
- Make meals and snacks as colorful as possible.

Eating a Rainbow

Blue/Purple produce, such as blackberries, raisins, grapes, prunes and eggplant, lowers the risk of cancer, and enhances a strong memory.

Green produce, such as avocados, limes, green apples, kale, chard, asparagus, broccoli, cabbage, green beans, peas, and zucchini, lowers the risk of cancer, enhances vision, keeps bones strong and teeth healthy.

Red produce, such as red apples, cherries, cranberries, pomegranates, raspberries, strawberries, beets, and tomatoes supports a healthy heart and lowers the risk of cancer.

White produce, such as garlic, ginger, cauliflower, jicama, and mushrooms lowers the risk of cancer, maintains a healthy cholesterol level, and a healthy heart.

Yellow/Orange produce, such as squash, carrots, corn, and sweet potatoes, supports a healthy heart, clear vision and promotes a healthy immune system.

Beverages

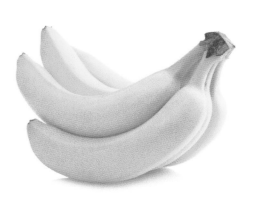

Carob Fruit Smoothie

Yield: 8½ cups

Equipment

Blender
Measuring cup
Measuring spoons

Ingredients

2½ cups raw cashews, soaked
4 cups water
4 cups cherries, fresh or frozen dark sweet pitted
4 small avocados
2½ cup coconut, unsweetened shredded
2 - 3 tablespoons carob powder to taste
2 teaspoons natural vanilla extract, alcohol-free
Pinch of sea salt

Directions

1. In a blender, blend all ingredients until smooth and creamy.

Fruit Art Smoothie

Yield: 4 cups

Equipment

Blender
Measuring cup
Measuring spoon

Ingredients

2 bananas, peeled and frozen for 12 hours
⅓ mango, peeled and cut in chunks
⅓ apple, peeled
⅓ cup of raspberries
3 Clementines
2 tablespoons coconut, shredded
2 cups water

Directions

1. In a blender, blend all ingredients until smooth and creamy.

Strawberry, Banana, Spinach Smoothie

Yield: 5 cups

Equipment
Blender
Measuring cup

Ingredients

3 cups strawberries, without stems
3 bananas
Small handful baby spinach leafs, washed and roots cut off
2 cups water

Directions

1. In a blender, blend all ingredients until smooth and creamy.

Salads

Brainy Avocado Apple Salad

Yield: 1½ cups

Equipment

Measuring spoons
Vegetable peeler
Cutting knife
Cutting board
Mixing bowl

Ingredients

1 avocado, pitted and chopped
1 apple, peeled and chopped
1 tablespoon raisins
1 tablespoon walnuts
½ tablespoon coconut nectar
1 teaspoon vanilla essence, alcohol-free
¼ teaspoon cinnamon

Directions

1. Mix coconut nectar, vanilla essence, and cinnamon in a bowl until well combined.
2. Add chopped avocado to chopped apple.
3. Pour coconut nectar sauce over avocado and apple and mix well.
4. Add raisins and walnuts, stir gently.

Corn Avocado Salad, Chipotle Dressing

Yield: 5½ cups

Equipment

Blender
Cutting knife
Cutting board
Measuring cups
Measuring spoons
Lime/lemon juicer
Mixing bowl

Salad Ingredients

3 cups heirloom tomatoes, cut in small cubes
2 avocados, pitted and cut in small cubes
4 ears fresh corn, cut off cob or 16 oz. frozen organic corn
½ purple onion, sliced thin

Dressing Ingredients

½ cup raw hulled sunflower seeds, soaked for 6 hours
½ cup water
1 tablespoon olive oil
2 tablespoons lime juice
1 clove garlic
3 tablespoons nutritional yeast
¼ teaspoon ground chipotle
¼ teaspoon smoked paprika
Sea salt and pepper to taste

Dressing Instructions

1. In a blender, blend all ingredients until smooth.

Salad Instructions

1. In a mixing bowl, combine all ingredients.
2. Pour dressing over veggies and gently toss to coat. Use dressing sparingly.

Kale Avocado Salad

Yield: 8 small servings

Equipment

Vegetable peeler
Cutting knife
Cutting board
Measuring spoons
Mixing bowl

Ingredients

1 head of kale any variety, shredded by hand
3 carrots, shredded
2 - 3 avocados, pitted and chopped
1½ tablespoons lemon juice
1 teaspoon sea salt

Directions

1. In a mixing bowl, combine all ingredients.
2. Massage and mix with your hands to "wilt" the kale and cream the avocado (this should only take a minute or two).
3. Serve immediately.

Sprout Salad with Hippocrates Dressing

Yield: 1½ cups dressing

Equipment

Blender
Measuring cup
Measuring spoons

Salad Ingredients

Organic sunflower sprouts

Hippocrates House Dressing Ingredients

1 cup olive oil
2 tablespoons lemon juice
2 tablespoons Nama Shoyu, soy sauce
2 teaspoons mustard seed, ground

Directions

1. Blend all ingredients in a blender or mixing bowl until smooth.
2. Drizzle over salad and toss.

Sweet Orange Salad

Yield: 3 cups

Equipment

Food processor, with a medium shredding disk or vegetable peeler
Measuring cups
Mixing bowl
Citrus juicer

Ingredients

7 carrots
1 cup of raisins
3 oranges, juiced
Pinch of sea salt

Directions

3. Use a food processor with a medium shredding disk or peeler to shred carrots.
4. Place carrots in a mixing bowl.
5. Pour orange juicer over carrots.
6. Add raisins and toss.
7. Add a pinch of salt for taste.

Side Dishes

Easy Guacamole

Yield: 4 servings

Equipment

Cutting knife
Fork for mashing
Lemon/lime juicer
Measuring spoons
Mixing bowl

Ingredients

2 ripe avocados, pitted and diced
2 tablespoons fresh cilantro, chopped
2 tablespoons lime or lemon juice
⅛ teaspoon sea salt

Directions

1. Mash avocado in a mixing bowl.
2. Stir in remaining ingredients and mash with fork until coarsely blended.

Pumpkin Seed Paté

Recipe created by Karen A Ranzi, www.superhealthychildren.com

Yield: 4 servings

Equipment

Blender or food processor
Measuring cups
Measuring spoon
Lemon/lime juicer

Ingredients

¾ cup pumpkin seeds, soaked overnight and rinsed
¾ cup white sesame seeds, soaked and rinsed
2 tablespoons fresh basil, minced
2 tablespoons fresh parsley, minced
1 lime, juiced
1 diced red bell pepper

Directions

1. In a food processor or blender, add pumpkin and sesame seeds and blend.
2. Add basil, parsley, and lime and continue to blend until smooth.
3. Scoop into a serving bowl.
4. Garnish with basil leaves, parsley sprigs, quartered cherry tomatoes and/or diced red bell pepper.

Sprouted Hummus

Yield: 1½ cups

Equipment

Wide-mouth mason jar
Cheesecloth, mesh or sprouting lid
Blender or food processor
Measuring cups
Measuring spoons
Lemon/lime juicer

Ingredients

1 cup dried garbanzo beans (also called chickpeas) makes 2 cups sprouted chickpeas
2 tablespoons tahini
2 tablespoons olive oil
2 tablespoons lemon juice
¼ cup water, add more as needed to thin
1 tablespoon cumin
2 teaspoons coriander
⅛ teaspoon of cayenne pepper, optional
Sea salt to taste

Directions - Sprouting Garbanzo Beans/Chickpeas

1. Rinse dried chickpeas and pour into a wide-mouth mason jar.
2. Cover chickpeas with 3 cups of water, and then cover the mason jar with sprouting lid or cheesecloth secured with a rubber band.
3. Soak for 12 hours.
4. Drain and rinse the beans through the cloth. Then drain again.
5. Store the jar out of direct sunlight at room temperature atop a kitchen towel. Lay the jar on its side with the bottom propped up so that excess water drains onto towel.
6. Rinse and drain the chickpeas once every 8 - 12 hours for 3 days. The tails should be the length of the bean.
7. Rinse and drain once more. If you like to keep sprouted peas for salads, air dry sprouted peas before storing in a container or plastic bag and refrigerate for up to 5 - 7 days.

Directions Hummus

1. Blend all ingredients in a food processor or blender until creamy.
2. If adding more water, add 1 tablespoon at a time until desired consistency.
3. Taste for flavor, adding anything extra you like.

Soups

Sweet Potato Corn Chowder

Recipe created by Joseph Lucier

Yield: 4 Servings

Equipment

Blender
Vegetable peeler
Cutting knife
Cutting board
Measuring cups
Measuring spoons

Ingredients

2 cups sweet potato, peeled and chopped
1 avocado, pitted and diced
1 tablespoon miso tamari
1 small knob of ginger, finely chopped
½ cup leek, chopped
1 cup hot water
Dash of sea salt and pepper
2 cups fresh or thawed frozen corn

Directions

1. Blend in a blender all ingredients, except corn, until smooth.
2. Taste and adjust seasoning if necessary.
3. Pour into a serving bowl and garnish soup with corn.

Cream of Zucchini Soup

Yield: 2 cups

Equipment

Blender
Measuring cup
Measuring spoons
Cutting knife
Cutting board
Lemon/lime juicer

Ingredients

1 cup zucchini, chopped
½ cup water, plus ¼ cup to thin if necessary
1 celery stalk, chopped
1 tablespoon miso
1 tablespoon lemon juice
Dash of pepper
1 teaspoon minced fresh thyme, save some whole leafs for garnish
½ avocado, pitted and chopped
1 tablespoon olive oil

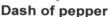

Directions

1. Blend all ingredients, except avocado and olive oil, until smooth.
2. Add avocado and olive oil and blend.
3. Add remaining ¼ cup of water to thin, if desired.
4. Add dill and blend briefly.
5. Pour into serving bowl and garnish with thyme leafs.
6. Serve immediately or chill for 30 minutes before serving.

Carrot, Sweet Potato Soup with Spinach

Yield: 4 servings

Equipment

Blender
Measuring cup
Measuring spoons
Cutting board
Cutting knife

Ingredients

2 avocados, pitted and diced
4 cups of water
4 small sweet potatoes, peeled and chopped
2 medium carrots, peeled and chopped
6 pitted Medjool dates, cut in half
1 teaspoon of sea salt
1 teaspoon of cinnamon
1 teaspoon of nutmeg
1 cup of spinach

Directions

1. Combine all ingredients, except spinach, in a blender and blend until smooth.
2. Pour half of the soup into 4 serving bowls.
3. Blend remainder of the soup with spinach and pour into the middle of each serving bowl.

Main Dishes

'Eggless Egg' Salad Sandwiches

Recipe inspired by Aimee Perrin

Yield: 3 cups

Equipment

Food processor
Blender
Mixing bowl
Cutting board
Cutting knife
Spatula
Measuring cups
Measuring spoons

Salad Ingredients

1 head cauliflower
2 stalks celery
2 dill pickles, pickled without vinegar
1 cup cashews, soaked
2 tablespoon lemon juice
¼ - ⅓ cup water
1½ teaspoon sea salt
1 teaspoon dry mustard
1 teaspoon turmeric
2 heads of mid-size romaine lettuce, washed and trimmed
Paprika

Mayo Ingredients

1 cup cashews, soaked at least 2 hours, rinsed and drained
2 tablespoons lemon juice
¼ cup water
1½ teaspoon sea salt
1 teaspoon dry mustard
1 teaspoon turmeric

Directions

1. Remove cauliflower leaves. Break cauliflower into pieces.
2. Add cauliflower into food processor and pulse until it's the size of rice.
3. Place cauliflower into a large mixing bowl.
4. Chop celery and pickles into quarter inch cubes and add to mixing bowl.
5. Add mayo ingredients in blender and cream it to consistency of mayonnaise. If too thick, add a tablespoon of water at a time.
6. Add mayo mixture to cauliflower and combine well.
7. Use romaine leaf as sandwich. Scoop a couple of tablespoons of "eggless egg" salad onto romaine leaf and sprinkle with a little paprika.
8. Roll up into a sandwich.

Zucchini Linguini with Marinara Sauce

Yield: 10 – 12 servings

Equipment

Spiralizer
Serving bowl
Measuring cups
Measuring spoons
Blender

Ingredients for Noodles

6 zucchini, peeled
3 tablespoons olive oil
3 teaspoon dried basil
1 teaspoon dried oregano
½ teaspoon thyme

Ingredients for Sauce

8 roma tomatoes, chopped
1 cup sundried tomatoes, non-oil, soaked
for 2 hours, save soaked water
3 Medjool dates, pitted
1 tablespoon lemon juice
Sea salt to taste
3 teaspoons dried basil
1 teaspoon dried oregano
½ teaspoon thyme
3 tablespoons olive oil

Directions

1. Peel zucchini, cut off ends, spiralize, and put in a bowl.
2. Cut noodles into 2 - 3 inches in length.
3. Stir in virgin olive oil, oregano, basil and thyme to marinate while preparing sauce.
4. Put all of sauce ingredients in a blender and blend. If too thick, thin with soak water from sun dried tomatoes.
5. Pour sauce over noodles and serve immediately.

Roma tomatoes are used because they are firmer and less juicy. Roma tomatoes are often called a plum tomatoes or Italian tomatoes they are commonly found in supermarkets.

Veggie Burgers with Ketchup

Yield: 6 servings

Equipment

Food processor
Blender
Measuring cup / Measuring spoons
Cutting knife
Cutting board
Mixing bowl
Lemon/lime juicer

Ingredients for Veggie Burgers

½ cups almonds, soaked for 8 hours
½ cups pecans, soaked for 8 hours
⅓ large carrots
⅓ cup sweet onion, such as a Vidalia, chopped
½ tablespoons of parsley
2 tablespoons of lemon juice
1 teaspoon sea salt
1 teaspoon rosemary
½ teaspoon tarragon
½ teaspoon mild curry powder
1 tomato
1 avocado
12 leaves of romaine lettuce

Ingredients for Ketchup

1 large tomato, chopped
½ cup sundried tomatoes
3 pitted dates
¼ cup water
¼ teaspoon sea salt

Directions Veggie Burgers

1. Add almonds, pecans, chopped carrots, chopped onions, parsley, lemon juice, salt, rosemary, tarragon, and curry powder to food processor.
2. Process until finely chopped and well mixed.
3. Shape into burgers using your hands.

Directions Ketchup

1. Place all ingredients in food processor or blender.
2. Blend until smooth, add water as needed to adjust consistency.

Putting it all together

1. Place burger on top of romaine/lettuce leaf.
2. Use slices of avocado and tomato as toppings.
3. Put ketchup on top.

Dehydrated Snacks

Cheesy Kale Chips

Yield: 1 cup

Equipment

Blender
Dehydrator
Mixing bowl
Measuring cups
Measuring spoons
Lemon/lime juicer

Ingredients

1¼ cups cashews, soaked for 2 hours
1 bunch curly, green kale
1 cup water
3 tablespoons lemon juice
1 tablespoon nutritional yeast
Pinch cayenne pepper
1 teaspoon sea salt

Directions

1. Wash and dry the kale.
2. De-stem the kale and break into two inch square pieces.
3. Put into a large mixing bowl.
4. Blend all ingredients except kale.
5. Massage blended ingredients into the kale getting it inside the curls.
6. Place onto a dehydrator tray. Don't worry about flattening kale leaves; they're better bunched up.
7. Dehydrate kale at 110° F overnight or until coating is dry.
8. Store in airtight container.

Cinnamon Apple Chips

Yield: 1 cup

Equipment

Mandolin
Dehydrator

Ingredients

3 organic Fuji or any apples
1 - 2 teaspoon ground cinnamon

Directions

1. Slice apples thinly on a mandolin, about ⅛ inch.
2. Lay apple slices in a single layer onto a dehydrator tray using a teflex sheet or unbleached parchment paper beneath. You may place slices very closely as they will only get smaller.
3. Sprinkle cinnamon over apples.
4. Dehydrate at 110° F for 8 - 10 hours or until apples are leathery.
5. Store in a sealed container.

Sweet Potato Chips

Yield: 1 cup

Equipment

Vegetable peeler
Mandolin
Mixing Bowl
Dehydrator

Ingredients

1 large sweet potato, about 1 lb.
1 tablespoon olive oil
2 teaspoons sea salt

Directions

1. Peel and slice potatoes on a mandolin, about ⅛ inch.
2. Place in large mixing bowl and use hands to coat sliced sweet potato with oil.
3. Lay potato slices in a single layer onto a dehydrator tray using a teflex sheet or unbleached parchment paper beneath.
4. Sprinkle sea salt on top.
5. Dehydrate at 110° F for 8 – 10 hours or until crispy.
6. Store in a sealed container.

Snacks

Ants on a Log

Yield: 15 servings

Equipment

Measuring cup
Cutting knife
Spreading knife
Cutting board

Ingredients

5 stalks celery
½ cup almond butter
¼ cup raisins

Directions

1. Cut celery stalks into 4 inch long 'logs'.
2. Spread with almond butter.
3. Sprinkle with raisins.

Halloween Witches Fingers

Yield: 27 fingers

Equipment

Food processor
Measuring cup
Measuring spoon
Toothpicks

Ingredients

1 cup almond, soaked for 8 hours
30 slivered almonds
1 cup walnuts
½ cup goji berries, soaked for 15 minutes
¼ teaspoon sea salt
1 teaspoon vanilla essence, alcohol-free
1 teaspoon carob powder
Few drops green vegetable coloring

Directions

1. Put all ingredients, except slivered almonds and goji berries, into food processor fitted with "S" blade and process.
2. Roll dough using your hands to make 'witches' fingers.
3. Put soaked goji berries in a food processor with a "S" blade and make a paste.
4. Place a slivered almond as a fingernail on the end of each finger.
5. Use toothpick to place goji berry paste around fingernail.

Desserts

Almond Butter Banana Ice Cream

Yield: 2 Servings

Equipment

Food processor
Measuring spoons
Ice cream scoop

Ingredients

2 frozen bananas
2 tablespoons of organic creamy raw almond butter
Water, if needed, to facilitate blending
Sea salt, optional

Directions

1. Peel and freeze bananas for 12 hours.
2. Break frozen bananas into chunks and toss them into food processor, along with almond butter.
3. Add a pinch of sea salt, optional.
4. Blend until bananas break down into a soft-serve consistency, adding one or two tablespoons of water to help facilitate blending, if necessary.
5. Serve immediately for a soft-serve style dessert, or transfer to a sealed container and store in freezer for firmer ice cream.

With only 2 ingredients, it's almost too good to be true. Naturally sweetened and dairy-free, this ice cream can be made ahead of time and stored in freezer for a quick frozen treat!

Apple Crisp

Yield: 10 servings

Equipment

Food processor fitted with "S"-blade
Vegetable peeler
Lemon/lime juicer
Measuring spoons / Measuring cup
8-inch pie plate
Spatula
Cutting knife / Cutting board

Ingredients

2 apples, peeled and thinly sliced
3 tablespoons lemon juice
2 apples, peeled and chopped
½ cup pitted Medjool dates
½ cup raisins, soaked
¼ teaspoon ground cinnamon
2 cups crumble topping

Ingredients Crumble Topping

2 cups raw walnuts or pecans, soaked for
12 hours and dehydrated
½ cup coconut, unsweetened shredded
dried
¼ teaspoon ground cinnamon
¼ teaspoon ground nutmeg
¼ teaspoon sea salt
½ cup raisins
8 Medjool dates, pitted

Directions

1. Toss sliced apples with 2 tablespoons of lemon juice and set aside.
2. Place chopped apples, dates, raisins, cinnamon, and remaining tablespoon of lemon juice in food processor fitted with "S" blade and process until smooth.
3. Remove from food processor and mix with sliced apples.

Directions Crumble Topping

1. Place nuts, coconut, cinnamon, nutmeg, and salt in a food processor fitted with "S" blade and process until coarsely ground.
2. Add raisins, dates and process until mixture resembles coarse crumbs and starts to stick together. Don't over-process.
3. To assemble crisp, press ½ cup of crumble topping into pie plate.
4. Spread apple filling on top using a spatula.
5. Using your hands, knead pieces of remaining 1½ cups crumble topping until they stick together.
6. Lay these pieces of topping on apple filling to form a cobbled appearance, allowing some of filling to peek through.
7. Chill at least 1 hour and serve at room temperature.

Applesauce

Yield: 4 cups or 8 servings

Equipment

Blender
Cutting board
Cutting knife
Lemon/lime juicer
Mixing bowl

Ingredients

8 apples
2 Medjool dates, pitted and soaked for 2 hours
1 tablespoon lemon juice
Cinnamon

Directions

1. Slice 8 apples and cut out core.
2. Place in a blender with dates and lemon juice.
3. Blend until smooth.
4. Sprinkle in a little cinnamon.
5. Pour into large bowl.

Brownies

Yield: 8 large, ½ inch thick brownies

Equipment

Food processor with "S" blade
Measuring cups
Measuring spoons
Cutting knife
Cutting board
Mixing bowl
Rubber spatula
Pan 8" x 8"

Ingredients

½ cup raw walnuts, soaked and dehydrated
10 pitted Medjool dates, soaked
⅓ cup unsweetened carob powder
½ teaspoon vanilla extract, alcohol-free
1 – 2 teaspoons water, if needed
Dash of sea salt

Directions

1. Chop ¼ cup of walnuts and set aside.
2. Place remaining walnuts and sea salt in a food processor fitted with "S" blade and process until finely ground.
3. Add dates and pulse until mixture sticks together.
4. Add carob powder and vanilla essence and pulse until evenly distributed.
5. Add water, if needed, and process briefly.
6. Transfer to a mixing bowl and add set aside chopped walnuts and mix well using your hands.
7. Pack mixture firmly into a square container and cut into one-inch squares.
8. Decorate each with a walnut.

Carrot Macaroons

Yield: 30 macaroons

Equipment

Food Processor with shredding disk and "S" blade
Measuring cup
Measuring spoons
Mixing bowl
Cutting knife
Cutting board

Ingredients

1½ cup raw almonds, ground into flour
2 cups carrots, shredded
¼ teaspoon sea salt
4 teaspoons cinnamon
½ teaspoon ground ginger
½ cup coconut nectar
4 cups coconut, finely shredded unsweetened
8 Medjool dates, soaked, peeled and pitted; keep soak water
½ cup raw walnuts, chopped

Directions

1. Shred carrots in food processor and empty shredded carrots into mixing bowl.
2. Change shredding disk to "S" blade.
3. Place almond flour, 1 cup shredded carrots, sea salt and spices into food processor and mix well.
4. Add coconut nectar and dates and mix until combined.
5. Add coconut, remaining carrots and walnuts.
6. Pulse together until blended.
7. Tip: If mixture is too dry and clumps together, use as much of date soak water until mixture will hold together.
8. Form balls with 2 tablespoons of mixtures and place on a dehydrator sheet. Flatten ball to make it look like a cookie.
9. Dehydrate at 115° F for 8 - 10 hours, until dry on the outside, but moist in the middle.

Lemon Italian Ice

Yield: 2 Servings

Equipment

Blender
Lemon/lime juicer
Cutting knife
Cutting board
Spoon

Stevia

Ingredients

4 tablespoons lemon
1 cup of ice
1 dropper of Stevia
Mint to garnish

Directions

1. Cut lemons into halves crosswise.
2. Juice lemons and add juice to a blender.
3. Add 1 cup of ice and 1 dropper of Stevia per each lemon added.
4. Blend until mixture is consistency of Italian ice.
5. With a spoon scoop out pulp from lemon rinds.
6. Serve Italian ice in lemon rind, garnish with mint.

Tip: Only put 4 lemons and 4 cups of ice into each batch to avoid overflowing.

Pumpkin Pie

Inspired by Joe Lucier

Yield: 8 - 16 slices

Equipment

Food processor
Measuring cup
Measuring spoons
9" pie plate

Ingredients Crust

3 cups pecans, walnuts or almonds, soaked for 8 hours
½ cup dates, pitted and soaked for 5 – 10 minutes

Ingredients Filling

2 ½ cups pumpkin or sweet butternut squash, shredded
1 cup dates, cut into pieces
2 teaspoons cinnamon
½ teaspoon ginger
½ teaspoon cloves, ground
2 tablespoons coconut nectar
¼ teaspoon nutmeg
¼ cup water, if needed

Directions for Crust

1. Process nuts in a food processor, until finely chopped.
2. Add the dates and process until smooth.
3. Pat down into pie plate. Cover sides with an even layer all the way to the top.

Directions for Filling

1. Place all ingredients into the food processor, starting with the pumpkin or butternut squash, and process until smooth and thick.

Assembly

1. Pour filling into piecrust.
2. Freeze for an hour then serve.
3. Pie can be kept in freezer for 6 months.

Raisin Walnut Truffles

Yield: 20 – 25 truffles

Equipment

Food processor
Measuring cup
Measuring spoons
Mixing bowl

Ingredients

4 cups walnuts, pieces
1 cup coconut flakes
½ tablespoon cinnamon
3 cups raisins
1 teaspoon vanilla essence, alcohol-free
⅜ teaspoon sea salt

Directions

1. Chop 1 cup walnuts in food processor until coarsely chopped.
2. Set aside in a bowl and mix with cinnamon.
3. Put coconut flakes in a separate bowl.
4. Put remainder of walnuts and other ingredients into food processor.
5. Keep processing until mass starts getting oily and sticking together. Don't over process.
6. Hand-roll mixture into 20 - 25 balls.
7. Roll balls around in chopped walnut mixture and coconut flakes.

Letters and Recipes by Real Kids

Dear, superinterdent
    I would love it if we
had more Healthy Meals
for lunch like smoothies
of fruits like Mango and Ect.
i will give you a list of foods
of vegtabals or fruits!!!

• Mixed salad with hippacrates
    Dressing.

• sweet potata chips.

• ninja smoother

• Ants on a log. P.S not real
        Ants.

Thank you for
your time P.s.
iam in 5th grade.
        sinceirly.
        Daniella L. Mendoza

← Back
For ingerdients

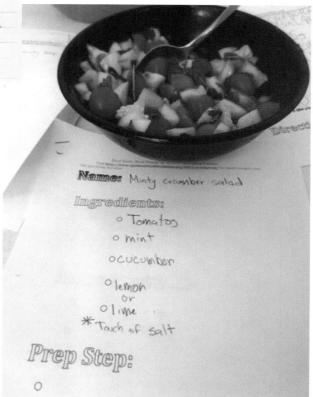

Name: Minty cranber salad

Ingredients:
    ○ Tomatos
    ○ mint
    ○ cucumber

    ○ lemon
        or
    ○ lime
    * Tach of salt

Prep Step:

    ○

Cummings School
Dear Ms. Bonel / Dr. Hatch,

Over the last 3 months, I was part
of a club at the Mystic Learning Center
called Real Kids, Real Foods. In this
club we made banana strawberry
smoothies with almond milk, Juices
with beats and apples, wacamoly,
Mixed salad with Hippocrates
Dressing, sweet patatos crisps,
Zucchini Linguini with Marinara
Sauce. These are things that i've
never had till now and I was
surprised how good I felt, right
after I had them. I don't
know if youve had drinks like
this before, but if you haven't,
may I suggest that you try
making a fruit smoothie or
a vegtable drink. And I would
like more healthy foods
available to me and my
classmates. They make me
feel good and what i've
learnd from real kids, Real Foods
how much healthyer these foods
are to me. Sincerly, David L.

Name: 2 TROBEBORAY
BANENISALD
Ingredients:
○ ORANG
○ MIN
○ 2 TROBEBRE
○ BANENIS
○ ARPL

Prep Step:
○ 2 LICE

Cross out prep step after you have washed or peeled your ingredients

56

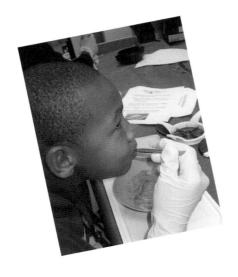

EAT HEALTHY!
FEEL HEALTHY!
BE HEALTHY!

Index